LOVE LOOKS NOT WITH THE EYES

There comes a time in your life when you focus solely on what

you believe is right, regardless of what everybody else is doing.

LEE McQUEEN

THIRTEEN YEARS WITH
LEE ALEXANDER McQUEEN

LOVE LOOKS NOT WITH THE EYES

BY ANNE DENIAU

ABRAMS, NEW YORK

THE MOMENT AFTER

Fall 1996. The fashion world was abuzz over the just-confirmed rumor that a certain well-known designer was leaving Givenchy to join Dior. A "young talent," as they called Lee Alexander McQueen, was about to take his place. I remember a PR person handing me a folder and asking: "What do you think of him?" There were only two pages in that folder; two pages torn from a magazine, that was all there was. I read through them. There were those two words, "bad boy," that would be forever associated with him, and a few photographs. I remember the water, models walking in water, black lace and a high collar that either confined or protected the face, you could not tell which. I remember a certain color, a slightly faded but still-sharp purple. I closed the folder and said the two other words that would come up again and again: "Strength and fragility. Both, extremes; it won't be easy."

I had been working at Givenchy for several months. I took photographs behind the scenes. I didn't watch the actual shows, I experienced them from the inside and tried to convey what I saw: the beauty of an ephemeral instant, the one-time event, the part that is rage and the part that is poetry, the fleeting, perfect, exact moment, the chaos that would normally have deterred me. There are no angles when you shoot backstage, no space for vantage points. It's crowded, the

lighting is harsh, and there is no room for error. That was probably what first attracted me; the impossible mission, trying to capture images that were as beautiful as they were improbable, small miracles that were not supposed to happen. I liked that, and being in the shadows: to be part of the process, even if you miss the finale. To watch something as it's happening, coalescing, reflecting the vision of a man and his team, the sound of the hammers setting the boards on the other side, watching trees and frozen underground scenery materialize, this confluence of energies coming together for one common goal, those fifteen short minutes, that was what I found appealing. Sketching out the traces, with dignity. I liked the panache, the craziness and the unbridled romanticism of a Galliano, so I was afraid I would not understand Lee. I was wrong.

In early January 1997, I was asked to follow him for two weeks while he created his first haute couture collection for Givenchy. A two-week time frame is both short and long. But it is long enough to establish a connection. Sometimes I translated for him. He didn't speak French, and very little English was spoken in the ateliers. That was not really a problem. It was in the *salons de couture* of Avenue George V that I first saw Lee take a piece of fabric and create a garment in under thirty minutes. I never forgot it. And I was not the only

one watching. During his four years at Givenchy, I witnessed the respect, joy, and admiration he elicited from others in the ateliers. Respect for the bad boy.

The exact date does not matter, I simply remember that the show took place on a Sunday. I was with him the night before. He looked at everything very quickly; his clear blue eyes never missed anything. It must have been about 11:00 P.M., and it was time for Eva Herzigová's final fitting: a white garment, part of the white and gold collection. Lee was not satisfied. He walked around her like an animal in a cage, he kneeled, stood up, took two steps back, forward, back again. He remained still for a moment, then said "Scissors," and started cutting. One sleeve came off, then the other.

(I am recounting events from more than fifteen years ago. I remember them perfectly. Recently, someone told me that "nothing lasts forever," but I have come to realize that memories can last forever. And forever is a very long time. Photography may feel optional, but it is not. It exists primarily as a means to transcend, then to share, transmit, or pay homage. In any case, that is how I worked with Lee. He understood my point of view, my outlook, and my vision very well. I knew that he was aware of what I was shooting at any given moment. If he said nothing, that meant he approved. For thirteen years, he never said anything. Only when I tried to coax him toward a quieter spot, with a softer background or a kinder light did he refuse. He would laugh, each time, challenging me, saying something like "Just catch me!" or "Catch me if you can," and run away. Naughty boy. One day, he was talking to a young model and he pointed to me and said: "See that girl? She's a great woman and a great photographer. Be nice with her." Be nice with her . . . Six or seven years ago, when someone told me I was his "protégée," I was surprised. Now, I understand.)

So, that Saturday night, he was cutting off the sleeves. It was less than twenty-four hours before the show. He finished cutting, put down the scissors, and gave some directions on how to finish, and he was done. The next day, he would enter the arena—there is no other way to say it. That night, we shared a cigarette. His clear blue eyes were fixed on mine as he challenged me: "So, what do you think of my work?" I am incapable of lying. I told him the truth, my truth: what I liked, and why, and what I didn't like, and why. "Yeah, you're right, that's crap, I failed." I felt the need to reassure him: "You're not fair with your work. It's not crap. It's unfinished. You're starting something. Give yourself some credit." He laughed. "It's done now. It's too late," he observed coolly. Beyond the windows, the sky had gone from blue to black.

And that was how it all started, on a January night in 1997. It was nearly midnight. We had spent two weeks together, day in and day out, watching each other furtively as truly shy people will. I believe we always felt intimidated by each other, for different reasons. So far away, so close. I loved him from day one, for his talent, which I will talk about, and for his humanity, which I will keep mostly to myself. I already knew that he was one of a kind. He would shake things up, and be subject to the insults, diatribes, and nastiness from the very same people who, years later, would call him a genius. The very same people. Sometimes, the fashion world has a short memory, but mine is intact. Indeed, in 1996, 1997, and even through 1999, articles were written, like damnations, about Lee's "British vulgarity," the "ugliness" of his face, the "brutality" of his manners, the "provocation" of his collections or their "misogyny." They wanted to take him down.

Meanwhile, I was watching him grow, take form, explode with as much intelligence as madness; "Sky is the limit," he used to say. I was immediately taken by his wild visions and his sharp mind but also by his tireless work habits, his countless trials and never-ending research. He worked relentlessly. Sometimes, ambling like a boxer, head down, he would bounce from one foot to the other, full of doubt, then full of confidence. He believed that anything worth doing was worth doing brilliantly. Sky is the limit.

The directors of Givenchy chose Tokyo as the next place to "launch" their new designer. That is where we next met, for three weeks, in May of 1997, following the prêt-à-porter shows that took place in March, in Paris. My assignment was to follow Lee almost everywhere: at work in the studio; during the fashion show, of course; as he made his way around the city; during a TV appearance; even at his hotel, where I discovered his down-to-earth side: "Can you play the piano?" "No, sorry, why?" "Because I have this indecent suite, with a piano, it's so stupid if you can't play." In June, circumstance prompted me to move to London. Soon after I arrived, he asked me to come work for him, to shoot his "Alexander McQueen" collections. I accepted straight away, it all seemed so natural, so obvious and fluid. This was September 1997. I could go on telling the story but in truth, there is very little to tell. I began working for Lee in 1997 and never stopped.

In 2009, we had our last long conversation at a quiet meeting in London: "I wanted you to document my life from the beginning, in your unique way; you have been the only one, and now you have my life in pictures. I trust you. I wanted it that way." He spoke about his face: "Imagine living with my face in this land of beauty! Fashion! It's love and hate, you know, every six months I want to quit. And then desire is back. And I work. And I'm happy, or proud. And I'm desperate, empty, and I want to quit again." And I replied: "I disagree, you're beautiful. Come on Lee, you're a grown-up! It's about time you give yourself some credit for this, too!" In 2009, nobody spoke to him that way anymore. He was treated like an idol. It made him laugh, that loud and luminous laugh. He showed me the costumes he designed for Sylvie Guillem, Russel Maliphant, and Robert Lepage, and we talked about my dear

friend Michael Nyman, whose music Lee listened to endlessly and had used in a couture show. Again, showing his drawings, he asked as he had the very first time: "What do you think of my work?" And I answered with the same honesty: "Mesmerizing." The fabulous costumes live on, and I suppose that many of us feel a sense of joy in seeing them on stage.

Lee Alexander McQueen.

How shall I describe him, who was known mainly by his middle name, Alexander? I speak more easily through photographs. Especially those he looked at, while I was shooting, and later, when I showed him the prints, mostly black and white. I know which images he liked, and why. Memories rush forth—it's terrible, it's an avalanche. I remember everything, exactly.

Photographs. This one, from October 2002, Irere, just a face, no clothes, no accessories: because he said it captured perfectly the spirit of the show. "Are you reading me?" he asked, often. That one, from March 2002, because he thought he looked handsome for once, and indeed, he cut a proud figure. I love everything about this shot: his regal stance, his beautifully cut jacket, of course, but especially his gaze, his concentration as he leans over a garment to adjust what for others was just a detail. Or this improbable shot of Shalom Harlow, arms slightly raised, as if she had just returned from a trip; yes, we were all returning from a trip, unsteady, like stumbling sleepwalkers awakened too suddenly. That was the show titled # 13, September 1998: Shalom was wearing a white dress that had just been savagely splattered by two metal insects. She remains untouched in this image, though, untouchable, desperately virginal, not really ravaged by the two-sided attack. Surviving it.

In 2000, when I left London, he said: "Have an exhibition in my boutique," and we selected that photograph of Shalom for the invitation. He asked me to shoot three portraits for the exhibition:

"Find a way! Make me beautiful! Hard work!" We went to his home. We were alone, I picked out the clothes, he was looking through the closets, it was a good moment. The first shot I took was pensive and slightly melancholic. Then determined, suddenly. The second one was intentionally blurry: Lee, purposefully striding across the living room. Yet, through the blurry image, you can still make out the light in his eyes. In the third shot, he is standing proudly in front of a door that was neither open nor closed. "Beautiful." Indeed. "Done!" He was pleased with the contact sheets and that was my greatest pleasure: to make him happy.

During this time I call "the time of innocence," I would bring him prints, silver prints or peculiar prints; a blue portrait—a cyanotype—that he wanted blown up, that hung in the London studio for a long time; an aquatint, "My Head on a Plate," that he wanted done especially for the anniversary edition of *The Face* magazine. I would bring him my photographs and he would say: "You gave me some pictures, take some clothes, take everything you want." I never took enough. He would point to the racks: "I said take everything you want!" When I didn't move, he would grab some clothes, choosing for me, men's clothes, too, "for some lover." I laughed as he filled my arms.

In truth, I don't think I can talk about his work, I can't say any more than I have already said in the nearly four hundred photographs collected here. How could words accurately describe his creations—the astonishing shoes, the clothes made of wood, raffia, or leather, the metal corsets sculpted by his friend Shaun Leane (to whom he said: "If you can make it small, make it big!"), the flowers imprisoned in silk, roses, roses everywhere, roses made of any material. Or the astounding hats, made of feathers, roses again, butterflies, hats created for him by his lifelong friend Philip Treacy, soul mate from the start. How Lee loved roses . . . I recall the expression on his face in 2006 when the orchestra played Handel's "Sarabande" as the last dress,

made entirely of roses and not quite finished, sewn together at the very last minute, left a trail of loose flowers along the catwalk, just a few, falling delicately to the ground. It could have been a disaster; instead, it was a small miracle. Backstage was full of ecstatic joy. Photographs tell stories and there is one of Lee, the ultimate perfectionist, backstage, spraying that very same dress with rose-scented perfume. I watched him invent fabrics, design original patterns, transform an antique Japanese screen into a garment, create dresses out of paper, wood, and crystal. Apply the same rigorous mastery of tailoring and suits— his first skills—to pieces that flow. Pay as much attention to every detail of the material, the trim, and the finish as he did to the majesty of the performances he orchestrated.

When the pieces for a collection arrived backstage, looking like strange ghosts dressed in black garment bags, I waited breathlessly to see the clothes that would soon be revealed. I would lean in, taking in every detail, every invention. The work was spellbinding. And then Lee would appear, out of nowhere: "Do you like it? Have you seen this? And that dress?" Always the same questions. He would point out a feature, a certain detail, and lead me through a labyrinth of wonders. If the collection was exceptional, which it often was, he was on fire, beaming; it was amazing to see him so happy.

Backstage was a magical place where new creatures came to life, new in the sense that they could never have been conceived of before he invented them. The flower-women that bloomed in Lee's mind, sensual women with proud breasts, determined women with exaggerated shoulders, incriminating cleavage, pants as fluid as they were alluring, perfectly cut jackets that redefined "elegance," coats that shelter, and dresses, so many dresses, dresses of such heightened and sublime femininity, that every woman, with or without a soul, deserving or not, has dreamed of wearing them. It made him happy: to see his

creations worn by women whom he admired, women who were strong. And fragile. Like him.

No, my words cannot truly describe Lee's designs. Nor can I do justice to his warmth, his generosity, his commitment to friends, like Kate Moss, who was suddenly ostracized by many, but idolized by Lee; a dreamlike creature floating inside a glass pyramid, a woman who remained beyond the reach of common mortals, an angel who had most certainly not fallen. Say all you want about leather, S & M, masks, witches, the dark side of the moon—all of that was indeed part of Lee's world, but that world was mainly filled with mesmerizing creatures, each one stronger and more courageous than the last, larger than life, fierce or bewitching, feminine and positively triumphant. Perhaps by dressing these women, he also protected them. He loved women; he was surrounded by women. His mom, Joyce, of course, and his sisters, and then Sarah Burton, Isabella Blow, Anna Whiting, Sam Gainsbury, Trino Verkade, Katy England, Amie Witton, Patrizia Pilotti, Annabelle Neilson, Kate Moss, Daphné Guiness, and countless others. He was happiest in the company of women; it was easy and safe. And women loved him as well. Because Lee was not an angel, he was better than an angel. Sometimes, after a show, I picked up things that had fallen on the floor, thinking: "Feathers from an angel"; and indeed there were feathers that were broken, trampled, and ruined. Were they traces or happenstance? I often felt the presence of angels in Lee's creations. They were passing by.

Let the images speak for themselves, because they are raw, sincere, and genuine, captured on film, from the first day to the last. I used only film, raw materials, and alchemy. When it came to Lee, there was never any question. The choice was obvious. I knew he was as sensitive to art as he was to craft, magic, and excellence, to the essence of things. One day, when we were backstage, he told me that he appreciated my eloquence: "I'm not saying anything here, I'm taking photographs!" "That's what I said!" and he laughed. Lee knew. Every photograph captures the other and oneself, in equal parts. You cannot escape who you are. Being a photographer is based on a tiny yet monumental factor: trust. Trust in the other and in oneself. And then, serendipity or good fortune.

I saw and yet I didn't see anything. I like to think and say that I never saw any of Lee's shows. It's almost true. In reality, I saw only one, Widows of Culloden, because the space was so small, the show had to be repeated in order to accommodate all the guests. Otherwise, I only experienced the shows from the inside. I only saw sets under construction, rehearsals, fittings, girls getting dressed, leaving, and coming back. The anticipation, the joy, the release, and the fear, the buildup, the palpable tension that grew by the hour and by the minute, the adrenalin, and the climax. I understood, with painful acuity, why he disappeared at the end of each show. Fifteen short minutes and it was all over, finished, delivered. A deliverance. A birth. After so much poetry and so much beauty, as sublime as it was wild, there was nothing left but emptiness. Oblivion. Over the course of thirteen years, when anyone asked me after a show, "Are you happy? Did you take some nice photographs?" I had the same weary answer: "I don't know." And I was sincere, I felt empty, hollow, with no memory of the preceding moments. I wanted only to disappear. Somewhere, outside.

It was from the inside that I watched him work, concentrating, sitting on the floor, oblivious to the activity around him. It was from the inside that I watched his hands make gestures that became so familiar I could anticipate them, gestures of infinite gentleness: both hands resting on a woman's waist. I know the exact look the young women had when he placed his hands on them, I could read their minds: They were proud, and honored. He held them for just an instant. Maybe he was checking the fabric, the space between the garment and the body, the vanishing distance between dream and reality. When he knelt in front of a woman to adjust a garment, move a pin, make a tiny correction, the gesture seemed purposeful, never menial. There was another gesture: his hand on the back of his neck, moving back and forth across his head, as if he wanted to prevent an idea from slipping away, so many ideas rushing through his mind.

Maybe this book could have been called *Two or Three Things about Lee*. Maybe Shakespeare's words, tattooed on Lee's right arm, said it all: "Love looks not with the eyes but with the mind." "Why?" I asked him fifteen years ago. "Why did you choose these words?"

"That's the only thing I know for sure," he answered.

Fatefully, I need to return to the present. Such a shame. It's been almost two years. I never liked the month of February. Winter always lasts too long.

Enfant terrible. Terrible. The word suited him. He made me think of Rilke and his concept of beauty: "The beautiful is the first degree of the terrible." Lee could find beauty even in supposed ugliness, a shocking beauty that was almost too much to bear. His idea of beauty was a "terrible" one, one in which the invisible takes over the visible and our reactions go beyond what we have seen. Like all those who seek to express what cannot be said, he had to share your feelings of dread, to expose what could not be revealed, to reach the invisible side of the world. Defiance, commitment, surrender, almost beyond human endurance.

After February 11, 2010, I anticipated the inevitable fallout, but not the extent of it. Very quickly, the legend began. And the noise. The rumors. Not just terrible, but terrifying. I was deeply saddened to see the legend come to life, a grotesque, monstrous, twisted legend, fabricated by people who did not know Lee. "What do you expect," I was told, "he was a public figure." True, and false, he was not a "figure." And what was said did not reflect who he was. Legend, *legenda*, "what must be read." Perhaps the word legend needs to be redefined. Those insipid, sensational, and empty words about him, all pointless talk. Lee Alexander McQueen: Everyone claims they knew him—that does not concern me; everyone claims they loved him—that disgusts me; everyone is painting an incorrect portrait of him—that revolts me. I watched people pose for the paparazzi, feigning sorrow with insincere tears. I heard loud voices, some who pretended to like him and others who were proud to dislike him. The ones who truly loved him just whispered, said very little or said it discreetly. As time goes by, I am appalled to watch the horrifying "legend" take over the narrative of his life.

Lee Alexander McQueen, who left us the night of February 10, 2010. The actual date of his death is probably incorrect. The official date was February 11. What difference, you might ask, and that's true, what difference does it make what the date was, but you see, it has taken me nearly twenty-one months to write the other word, "death." Other dates were recorded, dates that give structure to the mourning period, that define the steps along the way, the tightrope on which we all try to balance ourselves, tightrope walkers longing for a balance that is forever lost. A funeral on February 25, a posthumous collection presented on March 9, ashes scattered into the sea in June, a memorial service on September 20, and, finally, on October 5, 2010, a McQueen show without him, the irreversible proof that if life goes on, it does so badly. It keeps feeling bad.

I've been writing, some unseen words. I needed to spell out the facts in order to accept them, or just see them at first, face them squarely—as he did. He faced the truth squarely, beauty and ugliness, intention and pretense, defeat and triumph—before accepting the facts: Absence is a most faithful companion, steadfast, persistent,

never leaving your side. Absence, in the end, may simply be an inverted eternity, as breathtaking as that may seem. I have all the time in the world now, a brief eternity of time, to think about the infinite sorrow Lee must have felt on that day, February 10, 2010.

I have also all the time to wonder why I suddenly worried and needed to meet him, why I went to London and brought him that music, in January 2010: "Dido and Aeneas" by Purcell. I remember, I just imagined he would love everything: the music—almost sacred—the voice, and the singer. And he did love everything. He really did. On the ninth of February, Lee decided to have the singer, Simone Kermes, performing in his next show in March. A capella. Nobody would tell me why, and why. It's not a time to understand now; it is a time to reflect. And accept.

I'm certain that if I had to write about Lee freely, at full aperture, I would not succeed, I would not find the words. Indeed, I have nothing to say. In the logic of the absurd, the first and last of his shows that I covered were named Untitled. As if there were no exact words to describe him, no words sufficiently powerful, or subtle. Perhaps I would have to borrow the true, discreet, and simple words Sarah Burton pronounced in 2010, for no one could have said it better: "He was such a lovely man . . . You just wanted to make him happy." When you love someone who has become part of your life, you simply can't imagine life without him. Hard to grasp. The mind does not even protest because the possibility does not even reach the consciousness. You can't imagine the moment after. We are dealing with extremes. "A choice is a jolt," said Sylvie Guillem. That's where the problem lies. It was Lee's choice, not mine. When I can accept his choice, when I can fully respect it, I will have reached the moment after. Maybe.

I wrote his story with photographs, not words. Photo-graphs. So right and so true.

I wrote it using the light, his light. As I rediscover all these images, I remember everything. Today, everything is still vivid, as he is. His absence is a constant presence. I am waiting for the moment after. Meanwhile, I make this book, since I have to. I have immersed myself in these images as I would on a journey, a very long journey. Selecting four hundred images from more than thirty thousand . . . we talked about doing that. Lee would come to my home, we would spread the photographs all over, it would be so much fun. He asked me: "How much space do they take up? A suitcase?" I answered truthfully, smiling: "Two trunks, I suppose."

Two trunks . . . Paul Auster would call it "the weight of a man."

Sometimes, I'll stop and let my mind wander. Lee asked me once: "Where should I go diving?" "Inside yourself. It should be deep enough," I answered. He burst out laughing. Diving, a passion we shared. A handbag from his De-Manta collection. Atlantis. The colors of the ocean, transformed. The majestic gracefulness of the manta ray, the sharp elegance of a whitetip shark. A dress made of shells. The light that signals the surface. The escape. Water splashing on a face. Zero gravity, the source. In the mother's womb, in the ocean. And the silence. Then I resume my journey. And that is how I go forward, how I have done from the start. I just wanted to make him happy.

So far away, so close. Fifteen years. I feel it is important, essential really, to share these photographs. I regret, in the strongest sense of the word, to have waited this long. Today, there is a sense of urgency. To reveal. Lee Alexander McQueen. His Beauty and his Truth. To fulfill a duty.

It is too late. It is too soon. I am waiting. Waiting for nothing. Waiting for the moment after. I will leave the light on.

ANNE DENIAU
November 22, 2011

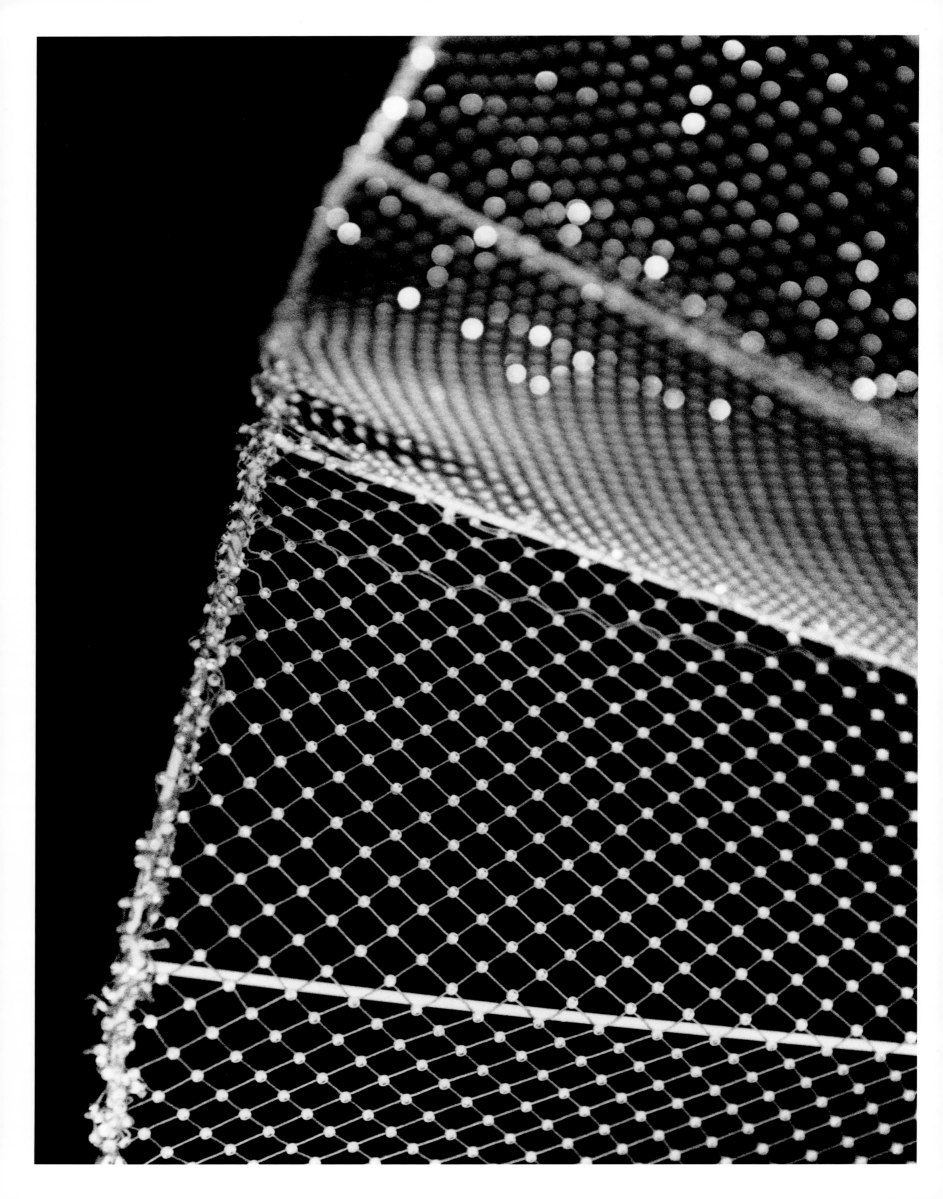

EGERIA

The time of effervescence.
Innocence.
Between September 1997 and February 2001,
eight fashion shows are presented in London, eight moments of grace,
including the mythic # 13.
Concurrently, at Givenchy, it is the era of Couture, of hours spent in Parisian ateliers,
learning, learning quickly. Learning, then forgetting and reinventing.
Lee Alexander McQueen, at full speed.
Joan of Arc is burning at the stake, the dark sky looms over women with darkened eyes,
the *salons de couture* on Avenue George V tremble.
In March 1999, Lee celebrates his thirtieth birthday in style. With good reason.
Nothing can stop him.
Following the Couture collection of January 2001, he leaves Givenchy
and decides to concentrate on his own brand, Alexander McQueen.
One final fashion show is held in London in a dark atmosphere.
The horses, dressed in latex, strike an arrogant pose,
but the merry-go-round appears to be spinning a little too fast.

UNTITLED

JOAN

#13

Lee was such an incredible man, a true genius, and his mind never switched off.
Every day he inspired and challenged me.

He made you think that nothing was impossible.
And you trusted him, since nothing was impossible for him.

SARAH BURTON, MARCH 30, 2012

THE OVERLOOK

FEBRUARY 1999 LONDON

EYE

SEPTEMBER 1999 NEW YORK

ESHU

VOSS

SEPTEMBER 2000 LONDON

WHAT A MERRY-GO-ROUND

Alexander McQueen took place in this world with a violence and a tenderness that I have rarely encountered. His physical presence, his energy, the palpable terrors that lived inside him (or where he lived!!!???), and his childlike, hearty, and generous laughter could fill any room. When I think about one image of his work, what comes to mind is a silhouette from his first collection (or one of his first collections): a bird of prey perched royally on the head, a hieratic body further elongated by a sheath dress, a corseted sensuality that was all the more blatant. The masterful art of mathematics, the opulence of history and the legacy of Gaelic legends inhabited his masterpieces. His work was admirable, truly startling, spellbinding; a synergy of the radical energy of nature, gathering the precious and precise subtleties of craftsmanship in

their quintessential state, and the mysteries of technology, invested with so much zeal and passion that it instilled a sense of poetry, heightened and unrelenting. All these adjectives and epithets, so clumsily aligned, could be attributed to Alexander, to Lee. For McQueen had guts and passion, power and charm, as in "magical" or "prodigious," a power filled with so much entwined virility and femininity, and childhood innocence as well, now eternalized, an inner fire that burned to the point of implosion, as if his body, his life, the world of fashion in particular, and the actual world were too small to contain so much visceral energy and unconditional anger. A fire that could not keep him away from the more fitting wide-open spaces of Scottish mythology, somewhere above Fingal's Cave and the Giant's Causeway, in full magnitude.

CHRISTIAN LACROIX, DECEMBER 14, 2011

GIVENCHY

1997–2001 PARIS

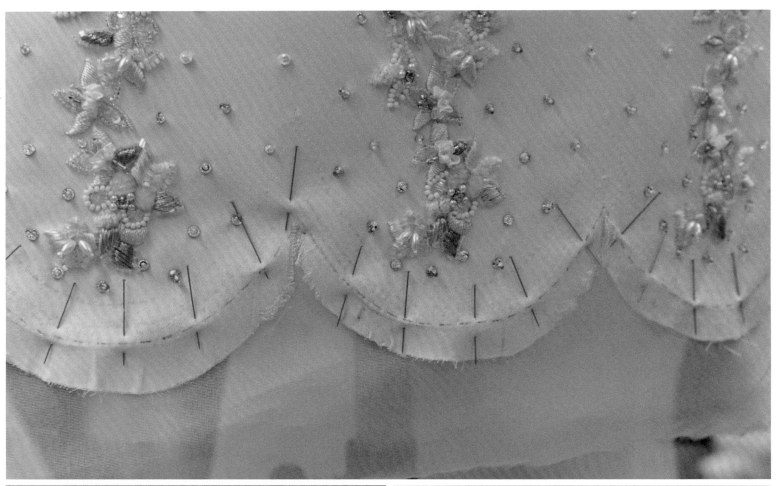

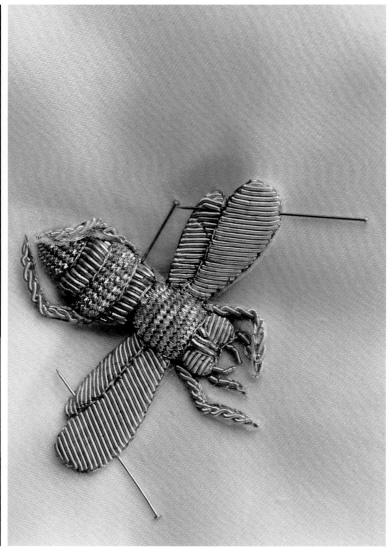

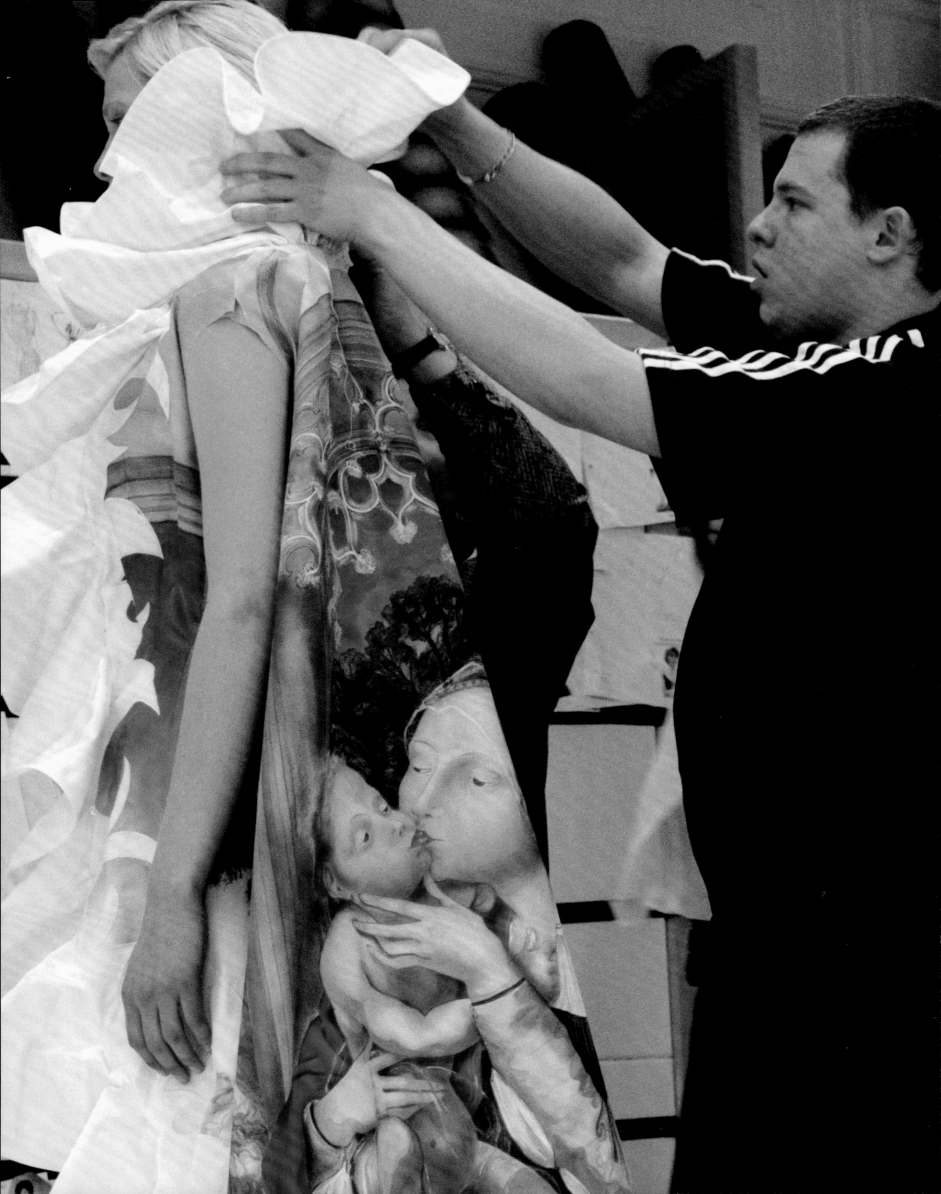

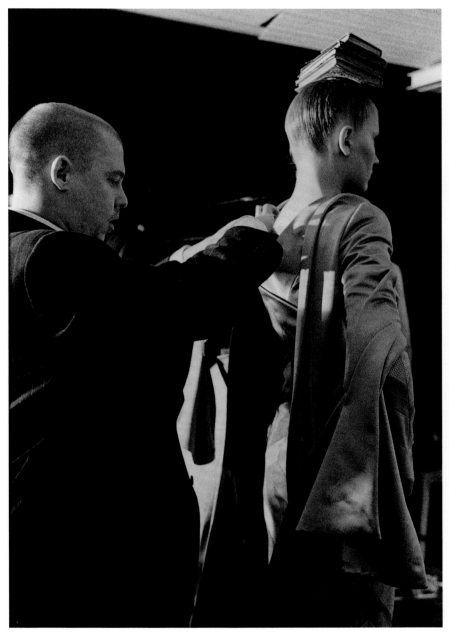

ALLEGORIA

The time of insolence.

Irreverence.

A brilliant tightrope walker, a determined man.

Lee Alexander McQueen does not move forward as much as he sprints along the wire. He is light-footed.

After the London farewell comes the moment of truth,

his debut in the most prestigious circles of fashion

and his show at the Conciergerie in March 2002.

Only one word captures the instant: "supercalifragilistic."

To mark the moment, Lee releases not dogs but wolves. The collection is sublime.

All bow to his genius, finally recognizing his immense talent.

The epic journey is just beginning:

an unforgettable marathon, a chess game, a glass pyramid, a sarabande.

The clothes are stunning and the staging dazzles.

"It's only a game," claims Lee. In this game, anything is possible.

"Sky is the limit."

THE DANCE
OF THE TWISTED BULL

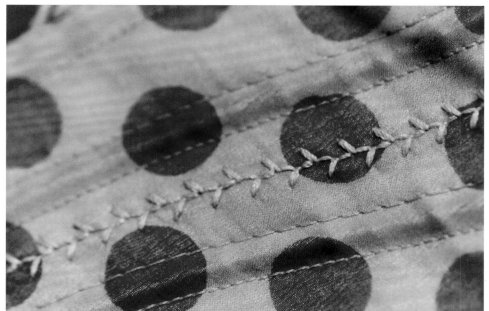

SUPERCALIFRAGILISTIC

MARCH 2002 PARIS

IRERE

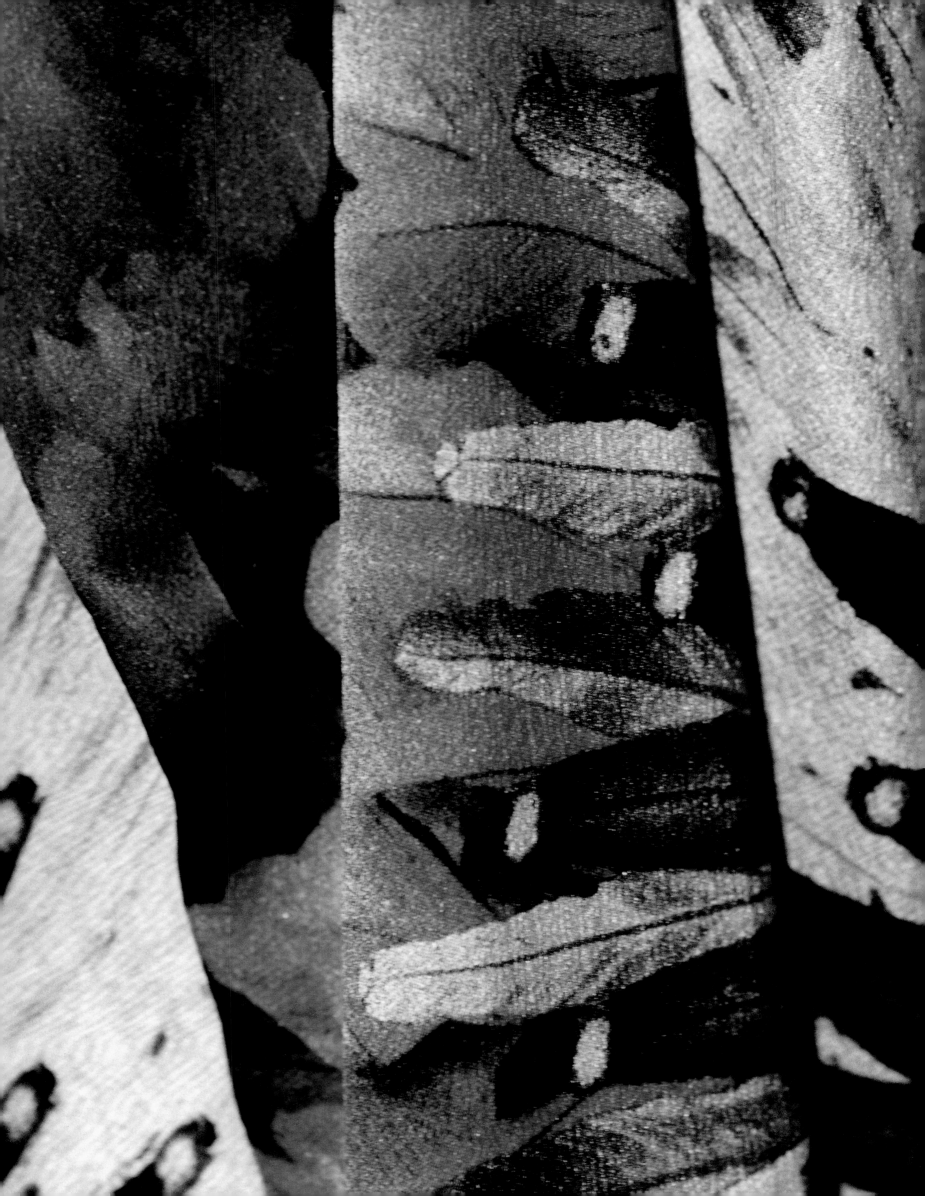

SCANNERS

MARCH 2003 PARIS

DELIVERANCE

OCTOBER 2003 PARIS

PANTHEON AD LUCEM

MARCH 2004 PARIS

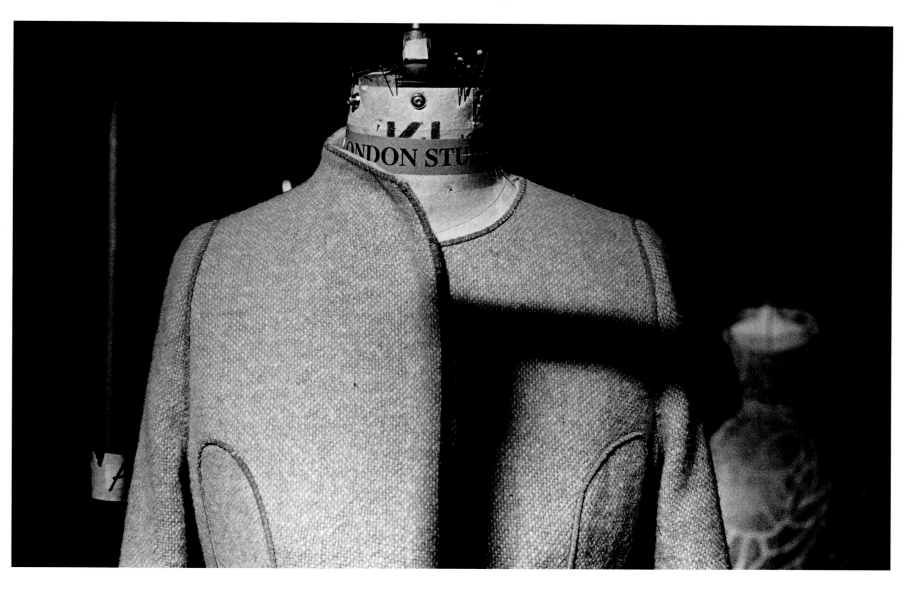

IT'S ONLY A GAME

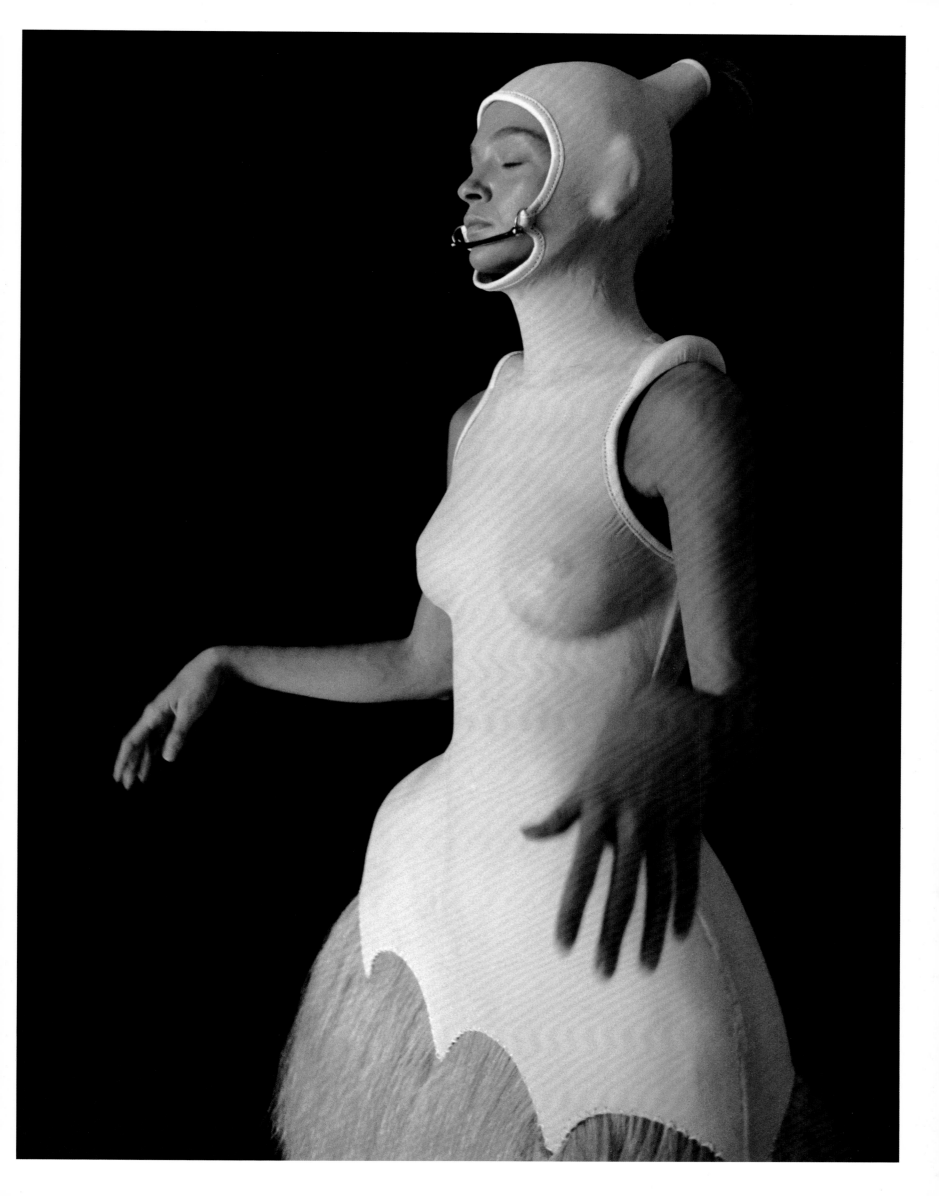

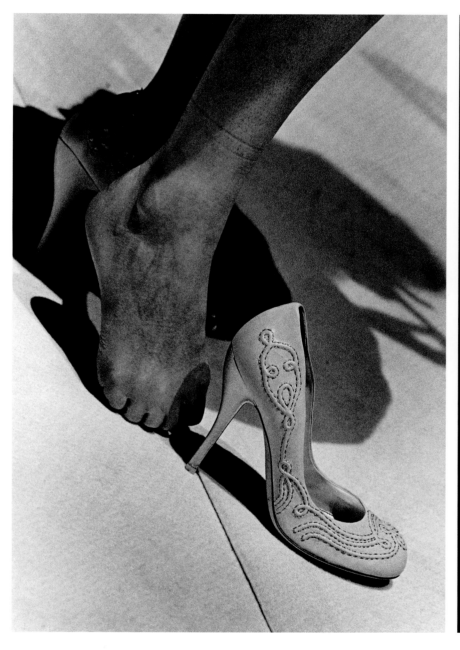

To have shared the love and passion of such a visionary artist
has given me the courage to be the person and designer
I am today.

SHAUN LEANE, JANUARY 20, 2012

I am so lucky to have known Alexander and to have witnessed
his extraordinary talent evolve and take flight over the years.
I miss him and his unparalleled genius. He was the best.

PHILIP TREACY, APRIL 5, 2012

THE MAN
WHO KNEW TOO MUCH

MARCH 2005 PARIS

NEPTUNE

OCTOBER 2005 PARIS

THE WIDOWS OF CULLODEN

MARCH 2006 PARIS

Everyone told me that Lee was a passionate and perceptive fan of my music,

that he first used for a couture show at Givenchy in Paris.

Lee told me so himself, a few years later, in my Islington house, when we discussed a new score that I wrote for him.

We did share mutual admiration.

The passion spread through St Paul's Cathedral

as I had the sad privilege of playing music from "The Piano" at Lee's memorial service.

Somebody is missing.

MICHAEL NYMAN, MAY 7, 2012

Lee (Alexander McQueen), the Little Prince from East London, fashion's enfant terrible . . .

Deep blue smiling eyes, extreme generosity, unparalleled genius, infinite poetry, magic fingers, and . . . the joy, the childlike happiness every time he created pure Beauty. His dresses were like clouds, his hats a world of fabulous fantasy, his makeup reinvented faces and beings . . . He leaves behind a great emptiness.

His universe of Dreams, of Poetry, and of Beauty was incompatible with our society, cruelly devoid of wonder.

We are left with what he imagined, we are left with what has touched us and the sad anger of having prevented an angel from taking flight.

His immense talent exuded a special light, the kind of light that our world deeply needs. A light that will be missed . . .

SYLVIE GUILLEM, DECEMBER 12, 2011

SARABANDE

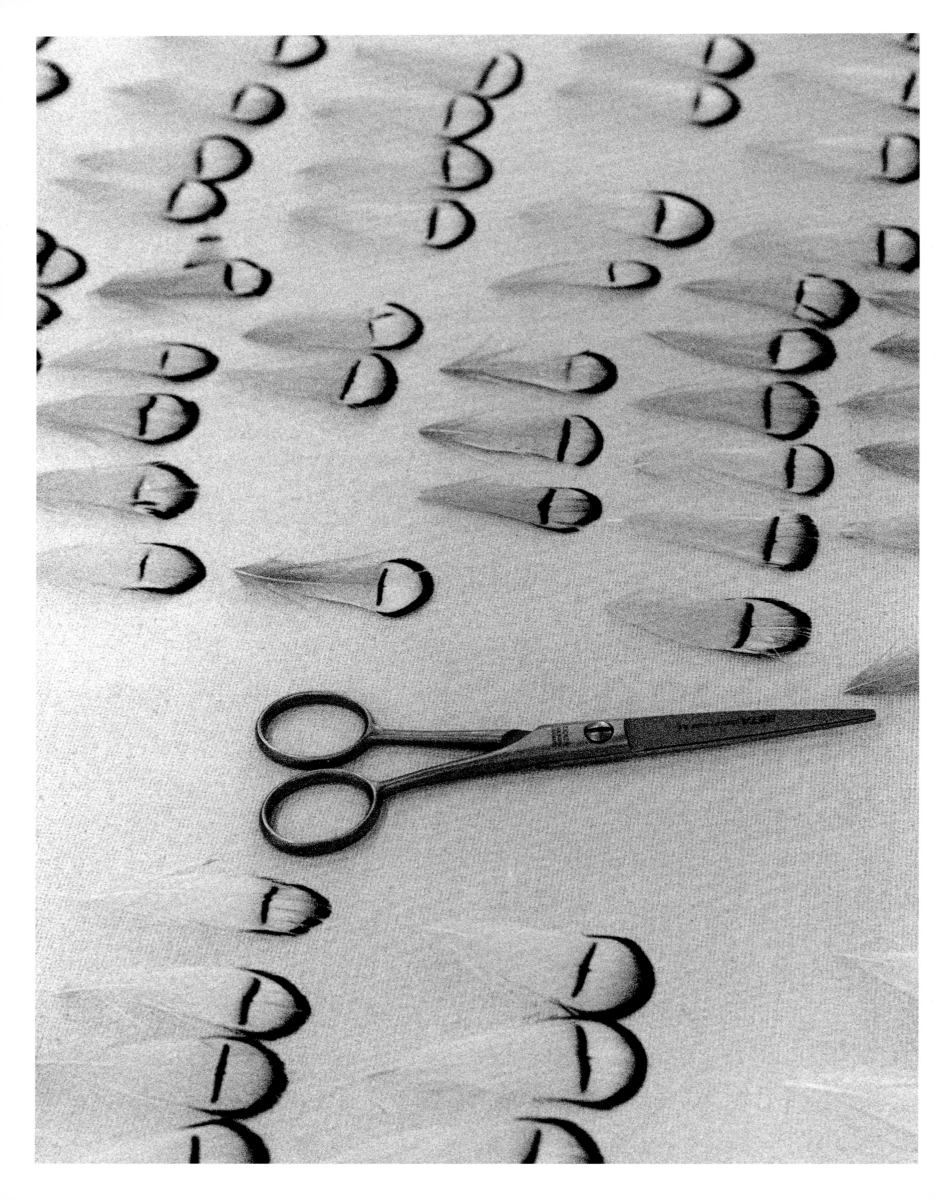

ELEGIA

The time of incandescence.

Evanescence.

Beauty at any cost. Beauty in the face of sorrow.

Isabella Blow, the trusted friend from the very start, dies in May 2007.

The mood of the March show was already somber and the October 2007 show is in homage to the lost friend.

Neon wings form a path of light for "La Dame Bleue."

Lee Alexander McQueen is flying dangerously close to Rilke's beauty, "the first degree of the terrible."

In March 2009, the set design, a pyramid of rubble, foretells the destruction of the past.

Sublime and disturbing creatures roam around the debris.

From their mouths, crimson silence or bloody screams. Black and white angels quiver.

The public is entranced, blinded, cheering its idol and pressing him for more. So be it.

In October, Atlantis, the deep-sea dive, proof, if needed, that Lee has reached the peak of his art form.

Against a blue screen, a drowning woman slowly moves her arms through the water

before going under, overpowered. Antinéa, perhaps.

Lee comes out to take a bow, alone, as most often, and slips away, quickly, too quickly,

to the debut soundtrack of "Bad Romance."

2010 is a year of grief.

On March 9, an angel folded his wings over a coat devoid of any color.

IN MEMORY OF ELIZABETH HOWE, SALEM, 1692

MARCH 2007 PARIS

LA DAME BLEUE

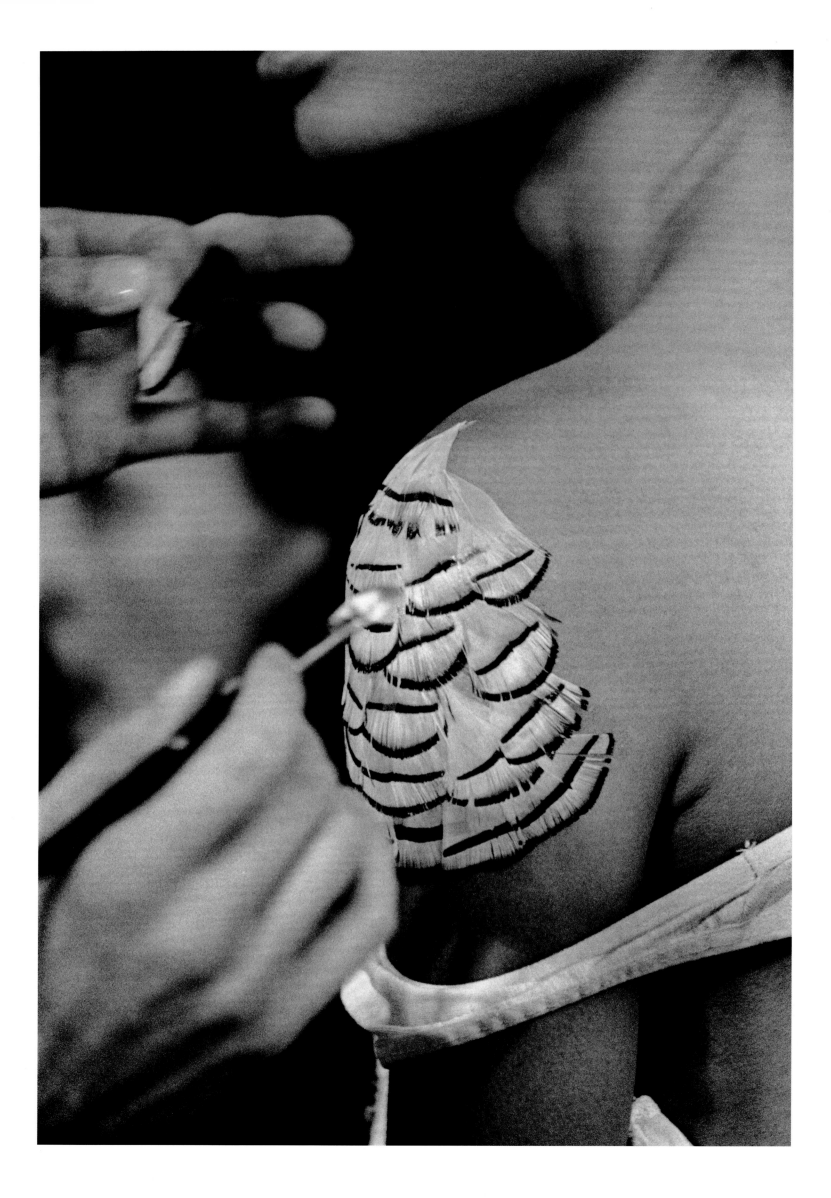

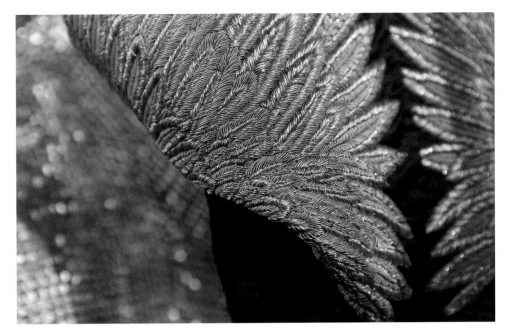

THE GIRL
WHO LIVED IN THE TREE

MARCH 2008 PARIS

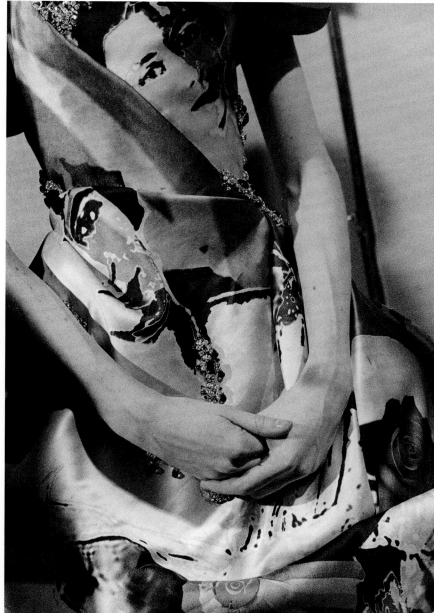

NATURAL DIS-TINCTION
UN-NATURAL SELECTION

OCTOBER 2008 PARIS

When I think of Lee, I think of the good times we spent laughing together.
He had such a sharp wit and made me laugh more than anyone else.
He was the most challenging person to work with, because his ideas were so inventive
and he constantly raised the bar and made those around him raise their game.
He also didn't care what anyone else thought: he was fearless and courageous
with a vision that was so inspiring and full of personal meanings.

He was a rebel with a big heart, who loved strong women.
I miss him a lot and all the great times we shared together.

KATE MOSS, MAY 3, 2012

Lee was an artist and a genius. He once said to me that if he ever left me I would know what this world was really like.

I already knew what the world was like, but without him now in it, it feels so much less, and I know he was right.

It was like an invisible wall that he had built to surround you; behind this wall no one could touch you, it was beautiful.

The last show Lee completed was the Atlantis show. We were in Thailand when the idea came to him.

Then he started drawing. He had drawn on several pages, but on four or five they were just drawings of a female form,

lying there on the table were we had eaten most of our breakfasts, sitting there, was this unbelievable drawing.

It was there straight away. It was perfect. I remember thinking that show was like he had found a new canvas.

I worry that time makes people forget about Lee, but I don't think there is anything I will forget.

All the memories with him are the memories in my life that I guard and treasure most.

ANNABELLE NEILSON, MARCH 31, 2012

THE HORN OF PLENTY

MARCH 2009 PARIS

PLATO'S ATLANTIS

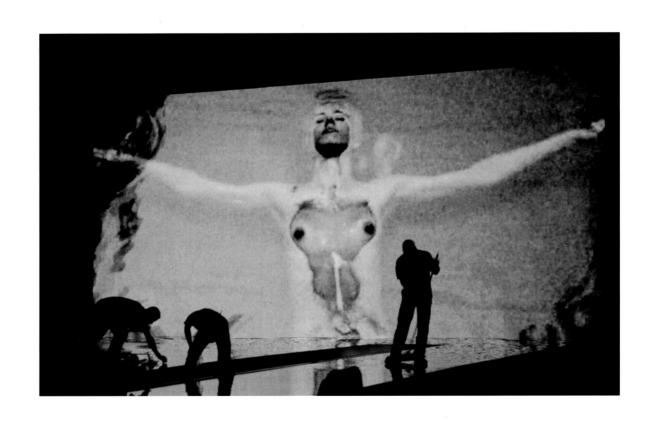

UNTITLED

Sky is the limit.

LEE McQUEEN

NAMES AND TITLES

ACKNOWLEDGMENTS

I send my warmest thanks to:
My dearest parents and my son, Tristan,
Lee Alexander McQueen, Sarah Burton, Sylvie Guillem, Kate Moss,
Annabelle Neilson, Christian Lacroix, Shaun Leane, Michael Nyman, and Philip Treacy,
Isabella Blow, for those precious moments we shared,
Carole Philippe, my beautiful friend, one of a kind,
Sylvie Guillem and Gilles Tapie,
for their tenderness on the 11th of February 2010
and unremitting presence while I was making this book,
Annabelle Neilson, Françoise Ha Van, and Shaun Leane, three guardian angels,
for their unique support, a source of inspiration and courage.
This book could not have existed without them.

I would also like to thank:
The model agencies City, Dominique, DNA, Elite, Ford, Idole, IMG, Major, Marilyn,
Metropolitan, Nathalie, Next, OUI, Silent, Vision, Viva, WM & Women,
and
Laure Aillagon, Sidonie Barton, Myriam Blundell, Myriam Coudoux, Gaïa Donzet,
Katy England, Sam Gainsbury, Alessandra Greco, Jess Hallett, Valérie Martinez,
Patrizia Pilotti, Selima Salaun, Etheleen Staley, Trino Verkade, Anna Whiting, Amie Witton,
Jonathan Ackeroyd, Hervé Caté, Didier Léger, Pierre-Yves Michel, Jean-Jacques Picart,
and the faithful Alexander McQueen team.

At Abrams I want to thank Ankur Ghosh, Sarah Gifford, Michael Jacobs,
Ivy McFadden, Anet Sirna-Bruder, Kara Strubel, Steve Tager,
and especially Eric Himmel, for his ultimate patience and kind understanding.

Art Direction by FRANÇOISE HA VAN

This book is fully dedicated to:
Lee Alexander McQueen, a lovely man who has gone forward and is terribly missed,
and Sarah Burton, who accomplishes with immense talent, dedication, and humanity
what Lee would have wished,
and beyond.

Cover Design: 2x4
Design Manager: Kara Strubel
Production: Anet Sirna-Bruder and Ankur Ghosh

Cataloging-in-Publication Data has been applied for
and may be obtained from the Library of Congress.
ISBN: 978-1-4197-0448-2

Printed and bound in Hong Kong, China
10 9 8 7 6 5 4 3 2 1

Abrams books are available at special discounts when purchased in quantity
for premiums and promotions as well as fundraising or educational use.
Special editions can also be created to specification. For details, contact
specialsales@abramsbooks.com or the address below.

115 West 18th Street
New York, NY 10011
www.abramsbooks.com